LIFE DEATH REVELATIONS

Bahareh Amidi

Life
Death
Revelations

ISBN 978-0-9974573-4-6

cover and interior illustrations by
  Andy and Dinka Nechaevsky

email: connect@bahareh.com
facebook.com/Bahareh.Amidi
twitter.com/BaharehAmidi
youtube.com/baharehLIVE
instagram.com/bahareh_poetess
www.bahareh.com

Listen to Life Death Revelations

a speck of dust in the hourglass of the universe

I resolve
I resolve to sit for a moment in the darkness
   of the early hours of this morning come
I resolve to sit, pray and watch my breath
Such Beauty in the Rhythm–
In and out—naturally—without effort
I resolve to be present
Simply watching the shadow of
   my pen on paper
The flow of Breath
The Beauty of flow
A sip of life
A sip of water
A sip of life
Here Now

Essence
Beauty
Resolved

It just occurs to me

As I think about the birth of my great nieces to come to the
world in the weeks ahead

And I also think about the sunset of my mother's life.

The Beautiful similarities of life and death had never
occurred to me before.

We are certain or hopeful that after a gestation of 9 months —
a child is born into the world.

For a natural birth we are never sure of the exact date

Sometimes the gestation period is abruptly ceased—and a
c-section performed—or a hardship may put a strain on the
womb and the baby is delivered into the world a few days or
weeks earlier than planned.

Nevertheless there is uncertainty and Joy

Similarly one knows that a person's average life span is around
80-90 years but one does not know the exact day.

At times lives are abruptly ceased with an accident
    or occurrence
Otherwise naturally life is ceased
For some reason- usually there is no laughter
    around death
Although in reality there should be joy—
    for we are returning to the source
    to the grand womb—to the Light
A baby is washed and cleaned off of the things
    on the body that helped in the womb but no
    longer necessary here-
A person's body after death is also washed as if
    washed off of the residue of life
The baby is wrapped in the blanket
    all covered and handed to the mother
The body of the deceased is also wrapped
    usually in a white cloth before the
    body is handed to the arms of
    mother earth

In reality the baby terminates life in the womb
and comes to the world for some worldly experiences
Let's remember the baby was simply a seed in formation—
in gestation
Here for a duration
Where was the child before
It feels certain somehow that the Being of that child always existed
in the universe and it was simply waiting for a body to be formed
in order to enter life.
So too when a person dies- they are simply leaving the body—the
vessel—some even say the cage behind
in order to experience true life in the arms of the beloved

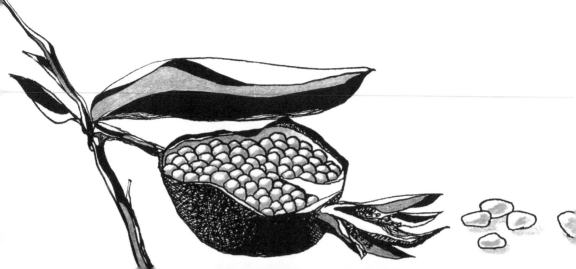

Washed and dressed in a cloth the baby enters the world
The baby cries—at first
But all others are joyous—those around
The opposite is usually the case in the case of death of a loved one-
Let's say even after a full life of 80 or 90
It occurs to me that the person who has just died
　　must be rejoicing as those around weep
Rejoicing for once again there is unity
Unity of self to thee
True essence of life in pure connection to
Light

The child stops crying as they latch onto life-
I hope to realize that
    when the eldest in my circle of family passes away-
    when mother dies
She is in pure Bliss and so why should I cry?
Yes I will miss her but she is with me always
She is in every Breath
    every wink of an eye
    for she is the womb that carried me here to NOW
    when she returns home
I must be aware of this Light in flight

Just as the baby's umbilical cord is cut from the mother—in order to
  prepare them for life here in this world—
So too the Breath must cease-
  the heart stop beating as it is attached to this space and time
The body left behind
The umbilical cord left behind
The body buried, or cremated or given to sea
All in all there is a cutting of cords with this
  life in order to arrive in Paradise, in Bliss,
   in the beautiful Pure return to Light
No Breath
But Real
Life

Just as it takes an infant
    sometime to latch on
    and learn the ways of the
    world
So too the newly departed
    must find the way–
The way to dance, the way to float
    the way to smile in the weightless world
    of space and time
    float and connect and latch on to life
    through Light
A new Life
Who knows perhaps another
    return to earth to find
    another home,
    another body and life

A new Life
The possibility of simply existing in the world of true existence
   which is living as
Light in Light
   connected
   illuminated
   floating
   existing
   smiling
Being
Divine
Light

A question occurs to me
What does the infant carry with them upon arrival into
   the arms of the parents
In reality
Nothing at all
Simply a Spark
It is the spark of life
The spark of Light
Does the infant carry a file filled with things to do
Or things it has done to arrive to here and now
No
And so as we depart—
We depart carrying Nothing with us—But the
Light
The Light of our deeds in our lives
The lighter we are
The higher we float-
The easier it will be to experience flight
   as a weightless speck of
Light

The infant leaves one world to enter the 'real world'
    leaves behind the small womb to enter the world
In the womb with limited things to eat and see and experience
    hearing things through the layers and layers of skin and tissue
    and such-always connected-nowhere to go-until Birth-
    endless possibilities of seeing, hearing, experiencing growing, walking,
    running, boating, biking, fishing, climbing reaching new heights
    worldly heights, and if aware looking within for true heights

So too the person who dies to this world is in fact flying
   to a world of no limits
No boundaries
Everything is grander
So grand beyond thought or belief
No borders
Colors iridescent and Light
Love pure and divine
True heights
Ones that do not limit a person
   to worldly goods or monetary gains
The essence of a
   human being in being human
Such truth revealed

The truth of an infant limited to the womb and the
   surroundings
The truth of us limited to here and now
For me my pen and paper
   the bed I rest on
   the clothes I wear
   the house I live in
The people that constitute my family and friends and few
   others-acquaintances and beautiful pure chance encounters
These are my truths

It is not for me to speak of the truth beyond—
    once my body has been washed
    and dressed in a beautiful simple
    cloth of white
But even the thought brings tears of Joy to me
    for somehow I feel the safe arms of thee
    welcoming me home—
    the seed in gestation I have been
Not sure when I will be ripened enough to
    fall from this tree of life
But the truth is….

The truth is…
There is essential Beauty in the return
   in the connection
   in the burial before flight
Wow the womb is indeed very similar to the tomb-
   enclosed, dark, safe, mother, mother earth
   hearing murmuring sounds
Not seeing beyond
But knowing deep down inside there is more than meets the eyes
The closed eyes ready to See

The Seal is Broken when the body is given to the ground
The Seal is Broken when the baby is given to the world
In one no more Breath in the other Breath with no attachment
In Both life and death
There is detachment
Detachment from womb and feeding cord
Detachment from world and family and worldly things

This detachment is key to survival-
The sooner the child detaches from
    mother-
        the sooner they start experiencing
        the world
I ask myself about my attachment to
        my mother, I feel this has all been
        an exercise in me letting go of the
        chain- or umbilical cord
Never the less- the detachment after
        death is essential
        for flight and for those left behind

And on one side the 9 months in gestation
The other side the 90 years of life
Then month 1 on one side year 1 on one side
Then month 2 years 2-10
Then month 3 years 10-20
Month 4 years 30-40 and so on....
Until Birth where cord is cut
Until Death til the last Breath
How Beautiful
Life and Life

And further more recall that when a child is born
   we know nothing about its world it has come from
We know not its thoughts or wants or not
So too when a person passed the threshold to Death or Life beyond
We know nothing of what is revealed beyond
All a mystery Before Life and After Life
Life is a certainty in the cradle and also before
In the grave and also Beyond Life

CPSIA information can be obtained
at www.ICGtesting.com
Printed in the USA
LVHW070852080322
712799LV00017B/77

9 780997 457346